The publisher of this book is generously donating all royalties from the retail sales of **"WORRY-FREE BANKRUPTCY"** to:

LEMONADE DAY

America was built on the back of small business. Entrepreneurs take risks believing they can realize their dream if they work hard, take responsibility and act as good stewards of their resources. Today's youth share that optimism, but lack the life skills, mentorship and real-world experience necessary to be successful. In 2007, founder Michael Holthouse had a vision to empower today's youth to become tomorrow's entrepreneurs through helping them start, own and operate their very own business… a lemonade stand.

Lemonade Day is a strategic 14-step process that walks youth from a dream to a business plan, while teaching them the same principles required to start any big company. Inspiring kids to work hard and make a profit, they are also taught to spend some, save some and share some by giving back to their community. Since its launch in 2007 in Houston Texas, Lemonade Day has grown from serving 2,700 kids in one city to 1 million children across North America. With the help of partners like Google for Entrepreneurs, Lemonade Day will continue to spark the spirit of entrepreneurship and empower youth to set goals, work hard, and achieve their dreams.

You can learn more about Lemonade Day by
visiting: www.LemonadeDay.org

I0040153

WORRY-FREE BANKRUPTCY

Conversations with Leading Counsel and Rapid Recovery Experts

By Remarkable Press™

Worry-Free Bankruptcy/ Mark Imperial. —1st ed.

Managing Editor/ Stewart Andrew Alexander

ISBN-13: 978-0998708584

CONTENTS

A NOTE TO THE READER

Thank you for buying your copy of "Worry-Free Bankruptcy: Conversations with Leading Counsel and Rapid Recovery Experts." This book was originally created as a series of live interviews, which is why it reads like a series of conversations that talk *to you*, rather than a traditional book that talks *at you.*

I wanted you to feel as though the participants and I are *with you*, much like a close friend, or relative, and felt that creating the material this way would make it easier for you to grasp the topics and put them to use quickly, rather than wading through hundreds of pages.

So grab a pen, take notes and get ready to learn some fascinating insights and real world bankruptcy experiences.

Best regards,

Mark Imperial
Author and Radio Personality

INTRODUCTION

"Worry-Free Bankruptcy: Conversations with Leading Counsel and Rapid Recovery Experts" is a collaborative book series featuring leading five bankruptcy professionals from across the country who are passionate about helping individuals and business owners.

Remarkable Press™ would like to extend a heartfelt thank you to all participants who took the time to submit their chapter and offer their support in becoming *'Get the word out Ambassadors'* for this project.

Remarkable Press™ has pledged 100% of the royalties from the retail sales of this book to be donated to Lemonade Day.

Should you want to make a direct donation, visit their website at: www.LemonadeDay.org

AMBER KOUROFSKY

Bankruptcy Attorney
AK LAW, PLLC

Email: amber@aklaw.attorney

Website: https://www.aklaw.attorney

LinkedIn: www.linkedin.com/in/amberkourofsky

Twitter: https://twitter.com/AKLAWPLLC

Facebook: www.fb.me/AKLAWPLLC

Accept Texts: (850) 284-6688

Call: (850) 284-6688

Amber graduated Magna Cum Laude from Florida State University in 2004, with a Bachelor of Science, majoring in Psychology, and minoring in Art. Prior to attending law school, she worked in Finance as an Account Executive at HSBC/ Beneficial in New York.

Amber received her Juris Doctorate degree from Stetson University College of Law. While at Stetson Amber was offered three internships, one for Judge Caryl E. Delano a Federal Bankruptcy Judge in the Middle District of Florida, one at the Community Law Program in St. Petersburg, Florida doing Family Law, and one at Ideal Image as In-House Counsel.

She also worked as a research assistant for the National Clearinghouse for Science, Technology and the Law, and achieved The William F. Blews pro-bono award for exceptional pro-bono work at Gulfport Legal Services.

In 2010 Amber passed the bar and was admitted to practice in Florida. In 2010 she was sworn into both the Federal Middle District and Middle District Bankruptcy Court. In 2011 Amber was additionally admitted to the Northern, and Southern Bankruptcy and District Courts of Florida and can currently practice in all Florida Courts.

Amber has appeared on behalf of Plaintiffs and Defendants, Creditors and Debtors, for a variety of clients ranging from multimillion dollar corporations to singular everyday individuals.

THE COOL COLLECTED CREDITOR
By Amber Kourofsky Esq.

Overcoming Obstacles

I help creditors recover debt owed to them in bankruptcy cases, so they can get what they are entitled to, and can be made whole again. A creditor is the entity owed money and the debtor is the entity filing bankruptcy who owes the money. Either can be an individual or a company. The objective in bankruptcy is for the debtor to rid themselves of debt, or reorganize it, depending on the chapter filed. Elimination or management of debts is the primary reason debtors file bankruptcy. When a debtor's bankruptcy is successful they receive a discharge of debt, and it legally eliminates a creditor's right to collect on any unpaid pre-petition debt.

How do you know if you are a creditor in bankruptcy case? You will know when an entity that owes you money files bankruptcy because you will receive a notice from the bankruptcy court. The notice sent by the court is called a notice to creditors. So, if you are the proud recipient of a notice to creditors, congratulations, an entity that owes you money is attempting to rid themselves of your debt.

One of the most common obstacles which prevents creditors from recovering debt in bankruptcy cases is for a creditor to do nothing. If you are a creditor and you get a notice to creditors, do not ignore it. A successful debtor legally prevents creditors from collecting on debts, permanently. Doing nothing only makes this easier for the debtor, which means you, the creditor, are left holding an empty bag. Worse, if you attempt to collect on the discharged debt, you, the creditor, may be sanctioned by the court, and be ordered to pay money to the debtor for doing so. Not fair right?

So how does a creditor know if they can collect and maintain their legal right to do so? The very real answer to this question is, they may not be able to. Sometimes there is absolutely nothing that can be done to prevent this from happening. However, the upside to this is that bankruptcy is very complex and there are many rules that must be complied with in order for the debtor to achieve a discharge. These rules vary depending on many factors, such as the type of debt, what chapter is filed, who filed, etc. Debtors frequently fail meet some of the lofty requirements, and as a result, their cases are dismissed. A dismissal can occur weeks, months, or even years after the filing. But ultimately until you consult a creditor's rights bankruptcy attorney, you won't know what your options are.

A second common obstacle is when creditors wait too long to consult a creditor's rights bankruptcy attorney. It is important to consult a creditor's rights bankruptcy attorney as soon as you receive the notice of the bankruptcy. Don't set it issue aside and "come back to it later." Time is of the essence. The reason for this is because, depending on the chapter, bankruptcy proceedings can move very quickly, and some bankruptcy rules contain very strict deadlines. If one of those strict deadlines is missed, then whomever missed it is probably SOL. And by SOL, I do not mean statute of limitations. This is why waiting to consult a bankruptcy attorney is almost as bad as doing nothing.

Regardless of what your perceptions of the bankruptcy process are, don't assume there is nothing that can be done. Alleviates your worry, and at a minimum, consult a creditor's rights bankruptcy attorney right away, as soon as notice is received. If the bankruptcy is filed anywhere in the state of Florida, you can always reach out to me.

One other common obstacle creditors face is not having proper support for the existence of the debt. One of the best things a creditor can do when lending money, extending credit, or for any transaction where they are to be paid in the future is to formalize the transaction in writing. Without a writing, it is very difficult to prove the existence of the debt, let alone prove any personal liability. Always put it in writing! Moreover, be diligent and contemplate the possibility of a future bankruptcy and incorporate pertinent bankruptcy specific provisions, verbiage, case law, or the like, in the written agreement.

It seems obvious enough, but many individuals, and some small businesses, often neglect to execute an agreement of some type. They do this for a variety of reasons, and I have heard them all. For example: I didn't think I need to, he/she is family; I never thought he/she would do this to me, I have known them since I was a child; I figured they would pay, they did in the past; they have plenty of money, I don't know why they won't pay me; I just didn't think I would need to, I didn't think it would come to this; etc. Although individuals provide rational reasons for neglecting to protect their interests, often times the reason stated is not the true reason. What my experience tells me is individuals often don't feel comfortable making someone, like a family member or close friend, sign an agreement. Don't make this mistake. It's not personal, it's business. If it is not in writing, it is very hard to prove it exists. Period.

My corporate clients on the other hand rarely ever have this issue. They almost always have a writing. The issue I run into with my corporate clients is the writings they have are insufficient or deficient in some way. Examples of this are when there is incomplete chain of title, or there is a lack of bankruptcy verbiage, or they have bad endorsements, etc. In these cases proving the existence of the debt is not the issue. The issue is proving their right to collect on the debt. So not only is it important to have a writing, but it is important to a proper writing.

Why is it important to have proper support for the existence of the debt? This is because creditors need to file what is called a POC (Proof Of Claim) in the bankruptcy case. This is the proof of the existence of the debt. A well written agreement goes a long way when proving a claim. If your writing is insufficient, the claim may be objected to, and you could find yourself litigating your right to collect. The case law for this issue can very complex, or "murky" depending on the type of debt and the chapter filed, and there are no guarantees a poorly written agreement will hold up if scrutinized by the court. If the objection is upheld by the court, the claim will be disallowed, and the creditor will not be able to recover.

Do yourself a huge favor and make sure your claim is accurate, and timely, and has proper support in writing! Try to include bankruptcy specific provisions in the agreement. The best way to accomplish this is to consult a creditor's rights bankruptcy attorney. Remember creditors who do this will be in a monumentally better position when it comes time to collect!

Helping Clients

Bankruptcy is code based law and is regulated by the bankruptcy code. What does that mean? In essence, there is typically limited "wiggle room" because the bankruptcy code dictates who, what, where, when, why and how. The code is a very large book and attempts to cover every aspect of bankruptcy, but where the code is not clear, there is case law for guidance. Since each filing is based off a debtor's distinct financial situation, bankruptcy is also very fact specific and because of this, review of issues often happens on a case by case basis.

I have helped many types of creditor clients recover money they are owed. One such type of client is the priority creditors. They are priority because the code says so. Priority debts are debts such as to the IRS, student loans, and domestic support obligations. Individual clients who are priority creditors often come to me as an ex-spouse recovering domestic support and/ or child support, and will have the most success recovering debt in bankruptcy. This is because this type of debt is largely exempted from discharge and the debtor has to pay it. For these creditor clients, I file a timely and sufficient POC. A timely and sufficient POC will almost always be enough to ensure the payments keep coming and that the creditor is made whole.

Quick tip - if you are going through a divorce and expect any type of future money payments, make sure it is clear that it is domestic support. This way you will be a priority creditor.

Other creditor clients I assist are secured creditors. These are creditors that have an interest in secured collateral, and are often financial institutions, but can be private holders. Mortgage holders and car loan are the most common secured creditor. Filing a POC may be enough to keep the monthly payments to secured creditors en route, however it also may not be. This is because the code, in some chapters, let's debtors manipulate secured debt. I help secured clients by either preventing the debtor's debt manipulation or making sure the manipulation conforms to what the code allows, and nothing more.

One such way to manipulate secured debt is by cramming it down. What is a cram-down? A cram-down is just like it sounds. It allows the debtor to cram-down the balance owed on a first mortgage or lien to what the value of the property is. Let's say, for instance, a property is valued at $50,000.00, but the secured first mortgage balance is $75,000.00. A cram-down will make it so the secured balance is now $50,000.00, and the remaining $25,000.00 will be discharged. This can also be done on other over secured property, such as vehicles. A cram-down will often involve a FEH (Final Evidentiary Hearing). A FEH is basically a trial within the bankruptcy case and will require appraisals, expert witnesses, and a good attorney.

Secured debt manipulation can also be done with a second mortgage or lien. This is called a strip-off. It is essentially the same as a cram-down, except the second mortgage is entirely stripped off. For debtor to strip-off a second mortgage it must be entirely unsecured, down to the penny. If the property is valued at $50,000.00 with a first balance of $40,000.00, and a second balance at 10,100.00, then the second is secured by $100.00 and a strip-off is not possible. In the same scenario, if the second balance is $9,000.00, then the second will be stripped off and discharged. As a result, the debtor will never have to pay it and the creditor can never try to collect it. A strip-off will also often involve a FEH, and will require appraisals, expert witnesses, and a good attorney.

I have also assisted unsecured creditor clients recover money in bankruptcy. These creditor clients will have the most difficult time getting what they are owed. This is because unsecured creditors are mostly the ones whose debts are discharged, in any chapter. That said, there are a variety of tactics I have employed to prevent a discharge, including but not limited to: bad faith objections, feasibility issues, and nondischargeability actions. But again, since each filing is based off of an entities distinct financial situation, and specific code provisions, this is evaluated on a case by case basis.

Common Creditor Misconceptions

The most common misconception about bankruptcy is that debtors think they can file bankruptcy and keep all of their assets. That is not usually the case. Pun intended.

When I first graduated law school I accepted a position with a Debtor firm. I consulted with hundreds of ideal chapter 7 debtors, each of whom had quite a bit of debt, were unemployed, and were falling behind on their bills. At first glance it made sense for them to file a chapter 7, until I dug deeper.

The fact of the matter is if a debtor has too many paid in full assets, filing bankruptcy can be a big mistake. By assets I'm talking about all the personal property the debtor owns, such as vehicles, electronics, clothing, money in saving and checking accounts, (not retirement accounts for the most part), bikes, guns, the lawnmower, literally everything they own, even the family pet. This does not include real property (homes). Having equity in any personal property is never good when filing a chapter 7, if you're a debtor. In Florida a chapter 7 individual debtor is entitled to keep $1,000.00 worth of personal property. This is called debtors exemptions. It is exempted from the bankruptcy estate and the trustee can't take it. Anything over that, they must turn over to the trustee to sell, or pay the trustee the value of the property to keep it. So if a chapter 7 debtor has a car, that is paid in full and is worth $6,000.00, the debtor is already $5,000.00 over their allowed exemptions, just with the car. Florida is one of the few states that has an unlimited homestead exemption, given the property qualifies as a homestead under the code. Florida balances this out by providing a minimal personal property exemption amount.

On the flip side, this is great for creditors! This is because if there is equity in it, the Debtor will be put in a position where they will have to either pay the aggregate amount of the value of those assets, or surrender it all.

The money paid by the debtor or the property surrendered goes to their creditors.

Using the car example above, exemptions work like this: If the debtor wants to keep the car, the debtor will have to pay the trustee $5,000.00 to do so since that is the amount they are over their exemption allowance. This $5,000.00 will be distributed by the trustee to the creditors. But the buck doesn't stop there! In addition, the debtor will have to pay the aggregate value of every other piece of personal property they have that they want to keep. If they can't pay for it, they will have to surrender it to the trustee to be liquidated for the benefit of the creditors. This is how chapter 7 cases become asset cases, and a surplus of money can become available to creditors for the taking. The only options for a chapter 7 asset debtor is to pay, surrender, or dismiss. Bad for the debtor, great for the creditor.

This is only for chapter 7 because chapter 7 is the liquidation chapter. The rules vary in other chapters, like chapter 13 and 11, which are reorganization chapters. In reorganization chapters the assets are typically in the form of disposable income, since you have to have a certain amount of income to be in one. Regardless of the chapter filed, or the type of creditor you are, at a minimum consult a creditor's rights bankruptcy attorney. There may be a way to recover money. You may or may not be made whole, but something is better than nothing!

Another very common misconception is that debtors think they can file bankruptcy and discharge all of their debts. This misconception extends to creditors as well. Creditors often mistakenly believe their debt will be discharged and there is nothing that can be done about it. It may be the case you will not be the cool, collected creditor, and if it is, then yes, there will be nothing that can be done about it. But don't start out with that mindset. As you now know from the discussion above, this is not always the case.

In addition to owning too many assets, another way assets become available for creditors is because they fail to itemize their property or undervalue their property. When debtors file, they not only self-value their possessions, they are the ones who list their possessions. They do this from memory in their attorney's office. Often times, things get left off this list, whether it be inadvertently or, in some cases intentionally. Cell phones for example are an item I regularly see not listed. Cell phones today can be very pricey and potentially, can use most of a chapter 7 debtor's exemption, and in turn, become a source for creditors to recover money. How does a creditor know if items are either undervalued or not listed? The creditor will know because their attorney will receive notice form the trustee, review the filing and discover it for themselves, or may discover it when the debtor is questioned.

When a bankruptcy is filed, regardless of the chapter, a 341 meeting of the creditors must be held. This is when the debtor is questioned regarding the information contained in their schedules (bankruptcy documents) by the trustee. This is not a hearing, but akin to a deposition. It is specifically for questioning the debtor. As a creditor, you are entitled to appear at the 341 and question the debtor. Creditors do not often attend the 341, but do if they believe the debtor is hiding something or if debtor fraud may be an issue. If the 341 has already been held, then an actual deposition will be necessary. In bankruptcy this is called a 2004 examination. It is much easier, and less expensive, to appear at a 341, rather than conduct a 2004 examination. This is one of the events that has a deadline and requires creditors to act quickly in consulting an attorney.

It is one of the trustees job functions to review bankruptcy petitions for fraud or asset concealment. The trustees will often get a percentage of what they distribute to creditors, so they are motivated to be thorough. I have actually seen debtors appear 341 meetings wearing expensive items, such as designer purses, shoes, and jewelry, which were not itemized or were undervalued in their schedules. I have seen trustees confiscate those items right then and there. I have even seen trustee's do this with engagement rings. The trustees took the ring right off her finger at the 341. This just goes to show you, you never know where or when an asset will be found!

Lastly don't make the common misconception of thinking you can do this yourself. Talk to a bankruptcy attorney. There are many rules and regulations, and they are updated often. So much so it is difficult for attorneys to keep up with them. But we do, which is why you should always, at a minimum, consult a creditor's rights bankruptcy attorney.

Navigating Pitfalls

There are all kinds of attorneys out there. Some will be good, but expensive. Some will not be expensive, but also will not be very good. Most will lie somewhere in between. Be aware that if you retain an attorney and that attorney fails to represent your interest, it is your responsibility to address the issue, quickly. If this is not immediately corrected, there may be grave consequences. A creditor, or any party to a case, who sits on bad representation risks ending up without remedy if the case goes sour.

Many non-attorneys are not aware of this, but in the legal system ignorance of the law is no excuse. So, when a party tells a judge they did not know, rarely will a judge take that into consideration. This is especially true when you have an attorney. If your attorney is doing a bad job, the judge will not have any sympathy for you if your choice of attorney is failing to represent you and you do nothing to fix it. The rationale behind this is since you freely chose that attorney, you chose that attorney's representation, good or bad. If your choice of attorney is bad, then you have to address it. You can't sit and let the attorney do a bad job and then ask the court to re-litigate the case because you sat and let your attorney do a bad job.

This is especially true if the case has progressed far enough to where "backtracking" the case to fix what your attorney failed to do may affect and/or prejudice the rights of the other parties. It's not fair to the other parties, and the judge will not prejudice them, so you can have a second go. Judges are gun shy to accommodate parties who failed to look out for their own interests, especially at the expense of the other parties. So the moral of this story is, be sure to do your due diligence and retain an attorney who is diligent, accountable, competent, and a good fit for you.

One thing to keep in mind when doing your due diligence looking for the right attorney is to be wary of any attorney who guarantees a win. No attorney should ever guarantee any result. Ever. This is true regardless of how strong your case may seem to be. Your position could be 100% in line with prevailing case law, but a judge could still rule against you. I have seen it happen. One time I was in court and witnessed a judge award money to a party/entity that was completely made up. What I mean by this is a typo in the pleadings created a party/entity in the case that had never actually existed.

Nevertheless, this judge ruled in favor of the non-existent party/entity and awarded them the money. I could not believe what I was witnessing. I am unaware of any statute, code, regulation, case, etc. that has held money can be awarded to a party/entity that does not nor has not ever existed. The takeaway here is no one, absolutely no one, can ever predict what a judge will do, and cannot guarantee an outcome. So I will repeat, be wary of attorneys who say they can.

One last thing to be cognizant of when doing your due diligence is that there should always be imminence in relation to dealing with a legal matter. However, the attorney or firm should never be overly pushy. If the attorney or firm is putting you in an uncomfortable situation and pressuring you to sign with them right then and there, be wary. There are firms that pressure people to sign for the fee, then let the case slip through the cracks. Don't put yourself in that situation. You should always be comfortable with your representation. I recommend when doing your due diligence to quickly consult two, maybe three attorneys. Consulting more than one attorney will help to ensure you retain proper, trustworthy counsel.

Stay Violation Fears

The biggest fear a creditor faces is possible stay violations resulting in court sanctions. There are only a handful of ways a creditor can violate the stay. Typically, it requires the court to find the creditor intentionally and/or willfully violated the stay. Courts can, and sometimes do, interpret intention broadly. For example, creditors who have simply neglected to stop automatic statements from being mailed to the debtor during an active case have been found to violate the stay, and as a result were sanctioned. This was not likely intentional or willful act of the creditor, but because of the creditors repeated negligence, the court decided to punish the creditor.

Stay violations are often the sole reason creditors are sanctioned. Avoiding stay violations is easy for creditors to do. One such way is to obtain relief from the stay. When a creditor gets relief from the stay, the creditor can no longer violate the stay. Once stay violations are eliminated, it's very unlikely the creditor will be at risk for sanctions. Not all creditors are entitled to relief and may have to use a different approach. The good news is, a competent creditors rights bankruptcy attorney should be able to advise on such matters.

Appearing in court for legal proceedings is another fear some creditors have. Fear not my creditor friends. The best part about being a creditor in bankruptcy is the sheer fact that if you retain an attorney, it is very likely you will never have to appear before the court.

What a creditor should fear about appearing in court, is not appearing in court. If a creditor fails to appear in court, the court could very well make a negative ruling against that creditor. To illustrate this point, I was in court and was shocked to hear a bankruptcy judge grant the debtor a free and clear home due to the creditor's willful failure to appear. The debtors owed well over $100,000,00 on their mortgage, but because the creditor failed to appear at two noticed hearings, the judge sanctioned the creditor the amount of the mortgage balance. This is an extreme example. I have only seen this happen once, so it is rare, but it has happened. Hence, why I have stressed the importance of not ignoring the bankruptcy.

Lastly, creditors fear the cost of representation will outweigh the benefit of representation. For the most part this is not the case. The cost to protect creditor interests is often minimal, especially if all that is required is filing a POC or simple motion, like a motion for relief from the stay. We call these simple matters routine matters. They have that name because they are routine and, in most circumstances, will be uncontested.

The only time cost typically becomes an issue is when there is additional litigation occurring within the bankruptcy case. These are called contested matters. The FEH for cram-downs and strip-offs mentioned earlier are examples of contested matters, as are non dischargeability actions. Whether or not the cost benefit analysis works in the creditor's favor in contested matters depends on the amount crammed down, stripped off, or in the case of preserving the debt, the amount of the debt being prevented from discharge (non dischargeability actions). Are the Debtors trying to discharge tens of thousands of dollars, or a few hundred dollars? Most likely it is the former and not the latter. Whatever the matter, your capable creditors rights bankruptcy attorney should be able to guide you through the risks and rewards. So, don't make yourself worry, and hire a creditor's rights bankruptcy attorney!

Rewards of Success

There are a range of reasons why a creditor may want to recover money owed to them by a debtor in bankruptcy. A very obvious reason is for the money. And that may be the only reason for some. This is the logical reason.

But for others, the reasoning can be very emotional. When I was initially contacted by Stewart and Mark, it was in relation to doing a quick interview segment on their "Let's Talk Bankruptcy" series. They asked me to pick a topic to discuss in an interview. At the time I happen to be involved in a bankruptcy case where an ex-wife was on the verge of having the bulk of the money owed to her, by her ex-husband, discharged in his bankruptcy. The circumstances of this case were such that when I was asked to pitch a topic, I almost immediately knew the issues of that case were exactly what I wanted to address.

In that particular case the wife had filed for divorce in another state. The husband did not appear or participate in the proceedings. All of the marital assets were in the form of the husband's retirement accounts. The wife obtained a divorce decree and final judgment and filed a settlement agreement with the court.

The settlement, for the most part, equally divided the marital debts, and assets. The husband did not sign the settlement agreement. The settlement agreement was, nonetheless, approved and ratified by the court. Ultimately, the debts were divided and both parties took their share of the debts. However, that was not what happened with the assets. This is because the husband did not pay to the wife any of the money in the retirement accounts. Pursuant to the settlement he was to pay her slightly over $100,000.00, to even out the distribution of assets and debts. This is called an equalization payment. However, because the husband had control over his retirement funds, he did not send her any of the equalization payment.

The wife's family law attorney added some bankruptcy specific provisions in the settlement in an attempt to make the equalization payment not dischargeable, but unbeknown to him, simply stating a debt is not dischargeable in bankruptcy in a settlement is not sufficient to make it so. As stated above, the case law in this area is complex and the requirements very specific.

This was particularly true in this case because the settlement was not executed by the husband. When the husband filed bankruptcy four years later, the wife was left with only a claim for an unsecured, money judgment, which is dischargeable. If the wife did nothing, it would have been completely discharged. After all the effort, time, stress, emotion, and money she had spent during the divorce proceedings, and subsequent to, she was about to have the bulk of what she was owed, discharged. This was her worst case scenario.

Initially the wife tried to represent herself in the bankruptcy. She did not contact me until over a year after he had filed. In this case, not drafting the divorce settlement in such a way to protect her interests in case of a subsequent bankruptcy filing, was her first big mistake. Her second one, waiting a year after the filing to contact me. Had she contacted me sooner I could have filed a non dischargeability action against him, and very possibly had her debt declared no dischargeable by the bankruptcy court, had her attorney fees paid for, and had the bankruptcy court approve a judgment with accrued interest.

This is not an option in all post-divorce bankruptcy filings, but it would have been in her case. This is because the husband's, alleged, activities during the length of the marriage were fraudulent in nature, and because of that she had a good chance of winning a nondischargeability action. Unfortunately for her a nondischargeability action is one that has a very strict deadline, which she missed. Luckily for her, however, it was a chapter 13 and the plan had not been confirmed, which at that point in time should have been. As a result, I was able to craft some unique arguments to get her payment through the bankruptcy trustee, which really was the very best result possible because I don't think he would have ever paid her anything otherwise.

Every case is unique. Whether a creditor's reasons to pursue collections are logical, emotional, or just for the principle of it, consult a legal professional. And do it sooner than later.

Why I Do What I Do

There wasn't any quintessential moment in my lifetime that led me to this path. Looking back, it was more of a culmination of events that pushed me there, many of them unfortunate.

I am a middle child of three girls. I was a fairly adventurous child. A free spirit. A tom-boy of sorts some would say. I certainly had an active imagination. I have, on occasion, been guilty of saying random, and at the time, to me, seemingly innocuous things, which in reality had the unforeseen effect of being quite the opposite. For example, when I was around the age of four, maybe five, I once asked my parents favorite friends at the time, "Do you know you have holes all in your face?" I, of course, didn't think anything of it. He was fun and cool, and in my naiveté, I considered him a friend. Also, it's not like it was a lie. He did have them. And they were all over his face.

I didn't understand why my mom was so mad at me on the drive home that night. I didn't understand why she said she wanted to crawl under a rock and die when I said that to him. It was only until after she explained it all to me, his embarrassment, her embarrassment, what acne scars are, that that I finally understood. This is but one example. My gem of a personality trait has changed over time, and has become more palatable, but personality traits are enduring. Although I have matured, I still have tendencies to be very forthright, albeit I have developed more couth in delivery. I think.

That being said, it's probably not necessary to explain why when I was a child growing up, I did not always get what I asked for. There were times I understood the reason. There were times I did not. One of the frequently given reasons why I could not have or do something was simply because I was female. This reason I never understood. If I am capable of it, obtaining it, and achieving it, being female should not in itself blanket bar it. There is something about being told that, to this very day, that lights a fire under me. Being impeded from the opportunity to obtain something I want, because I am female, is very, very motivating.

Throughout history there have been many theorists who have studied motivation. Some are well-known and considered some of the best minds of all time, such as Plato who brought his reason, spirit and appetite to the table (Plato's tripartite theory of the soul), and Freud who could think on his feet and in his sleep, (Freud's conscious and unconscious motivations). Some are lesser known, like Piers Steel who can synthesize primary aspects of several major motivational theories into one single formulation, (Steel's temporal motivation theory). Arguably, however, no one stroke of genius has fully flushed out the mystery that is motivation. The exact driving force behind the intrinsic impulse continues to elude even the greatest of minds today. I say find what motivates you and run with it!

For me, motivation is possibilities and opportunities. Motivation creates possibilities. Motivation is the possibility of achieving the greatest of goals. It is the possibility to contribute something great to this country, or who knows, even the world. The possibilities are endless if you can see them. If you want them. They are not handouts, given away at a whim. Some get lucky, sure, but most need to pay attention.

Motivation is the possibility of grabbing ahold of your fundamentally intrinsic instinct and taking those possibilities on a journey of a lifetime, over, and over, and over again. Allowing yourself to indulge in possibilities breeds opportunities. Opportunities can be boundless, but beware, they come devoid of warranties of any kind. There are no full satisfaction guarantees. There is no promise that you won't get hurt, or that you'll get another chance. Nonetheless, you must go. The opportunity is now. It's here right in front of you beckoning you to take it, and time is of the essence. The opportunity may not arise again. It will not last forever. It is fleeting, and it too shall pass. Your venture will someday end, so don't hesitate, ride that wave into the sunset. Otherwise you'll find you have been left, left behind, left with nothing. No hope, no living, no life.

It is up to you to create your possibilities and seize your opportunities. Take them by the horns. Steer them to where you want to go. Stay alert. Know when the opportunity is present. Be the architect of your possibilities and the navigator of your opportunities. Be the commander of your will. Have an exciting and fulfilling life. Feel alive. Live.

You only get to live once. This was something I was well aware of at a very young age. Something else I was aware of at a very young age was that most people's regrets in life were not of things that they had done, but of things they had not done, or not tried to do. I know this because for whatever reason whenever I was around an elderly person I always would ask them their biggest regrets in life. Rarely did any of them respond to my inquiry with something they did in life. Although I thought some of them should have because I was aware of some of the things that they had done, but ultimately those particular individuals reinforced my conclusion that, generally, not doing something you want to, was infinitely worse than doing something that maybe you did not want to.

I left home only a few weeks after turning 18. I moved pretty far from my parents in upstate New York, several states away... I had moved with my best friend from high school because she asked, and because her father had bought her a house, a three bedroom A-frame house in a private community on an island off the coast of North Carolina. He lived there and wanted her closer. What 18-year-old who grew up in upstate New York would say no to that? I sure didn't. I only lasted about a year on that island.

It only took a few months for things to take a turn for the worse. One day her father called me and threatened to kick me out of the house. He told me didn't like that I had a boy over to the house and that I was not authorized to do so on the future. He actually threatened to come over and throw my stuff out onto the street if I did not comply with his rules and demands. I was flabbergasted. I couldn't believe it. I may have been young, but I was not naive, and I knew he could not just throw me out. I told my friend about the situation, but she wanted nothing to do with it. I guess in her mind there was no point risking daddy getting mad and her for my sake, especially since her boyfriend spent just about every night there and she did not want him to say something about it or worse, stop paying for everything for her. She actually put her hands up in the air, told me it was between me and her dad, and walked away. She completely abandoned me. I felt so alone. I ended up calling the police on him because I did not know what else to do. I sure didn't want him to come and throw all me out into the street.

At this point I decided I was going to have to find somewhere else to live. So, one night shortly afterwards I packed up and moved out. I didn't know what the next handful of months yielded for me, but I was going to find out. Turns out, things got pretty hard. I had nowhere to go. I knew almost absolutely no one. I struggled to make it work for quite a while. I found myself living in a few questionable situations. Situations I would never want my 18-year-old daughter in. Living in random rooms and houses, and with random people. I ended up having to call the cops on two other landlords that year. There was even one point, for a few weeks, I had to live in my old Pontiac Bonneville. It's funny that my high school classmates joked on me about buying that Bonneville because it was one of those old timer boat type of cars, but boy was I glad, at the time, I hadn't bought a geo metro or a Honda del sol! I eventually ended up giving that Bonneville away for a ride home and a meal at McDonalds.

In a way Florida saved me. When I left that island, I did not go back to NY, I found my way to Tallahassee. Had I not left the island there is no telling what would have happened. People always tell me I am lucky. I believe that to be true. After all, I did win a brand new truck in a Nascar sweepstakes once. True story. But what people don't realize is that luck doesn't always matriculate itself in a good way. I've had my share of bad luck too. They say what doesn't kill you makes you stronger. That may be true, to an extent. I believe what doesn't kill you, doesn't kill you, but it sure will weigh on you and you will drag this weight around with you everywhere you go. Some call it baggage, but it is much more than that. Some things are greater than the whole of the parts from which they are made. This weight is one of those things. This weight is greater than the whole of the parts from which it is made, and as time passes, this weight has the potential to slowly eat away at you. This great weight comprised of all those things which didn't kill you, and all of the collateral effects of carrying that around with you, will eventually turn a person desirous. Being desirous can be a bad thing. It can go dark. It can go really dark. But it also can be the best thing that ever happened to you. Your most real life experiences stem from the desire created from your weight. Being desirous can be that thing that pushes you to be what you never dreamed you'd become.

Being desirous can give you the will to not just survive, but to crush your highest expectations. I know this to be true because that is exactly what my desirous weight did to me.

Final Thoughts

My top five reasons to take a notice to creditors seriously: (1) don't assume the cost will outweigh the benefit - it is very probable the benefit will be well worth the cost; (2) don't fret about a time commitment - it may not require much of a time commitment, for a creditor in bankruptcy a little bit of time can go a very long way; (3) don't simply do what the others did - what may be good for the goose may not be good for the gander, so just because the goose failed to respond, does not mean the gander should make the same mistake; (4) if you don't ask, you just won't know - how do you know if there is the ability to collect if you don't at least ask; and (5) representing yourself is a bad idea - there is a reason why attorneys have to go to law school, because the practice of law is hard, consult an attorney.

The long and the short of it is - at the end of the day, you don't know, until you know. If you ask, you may find yourself on the receiving end of things, and then you will be the cool, collected creditor!

Next Steps

My contact information is also at the beginning of this chapter, but if anything changes, all you have to do to find me is Google me, or you can simply send an email to: amber@aklaw.attorney. Please try to include some pertinent information, such as a case number, or even attach a copy of the docket and/or notice you received.

One of the first things people ask when they contact me is what I will charge them for representation, and understandably so. Unless your matter is a routine matter, my typical response is that I need more information. It is difficult to evaluate the level of involvement necessary in a case, without, at a minimum, taking a quick glance at it. I will take a quick look at your case and give you an idea of what may be involved and provide you a quote.

CAROL LYNN WOLFRAM

Bankruptcy Attorney
The Law Office of Carol Lynn Wolfram

Email: carol@clwolframlegal.com

Email: clwolframlegal@gmail.com

Website: https://www.clwolframlegal.com

LinkedIn: https://linkedin.com/in/carolwolfram

Avvo Attorney Profile: Carol Lynn Wolfram

Call: (940) 321-0019 | **Fax:** (940) 497-1143

Carol Lynn Wolfram was born and reared in Amarillo, Texas. She grew up in a family of lawyers and first began thinking of becoming a lawyer when she was about 12 years old. She received encouragement and help from her parents to go to law school at Texas Tech School of Law in Lubbock, Texas, but also worked all through undergraduate college and law school, including working at a slaughterhouse, a bakery, and waiting tables at a pizza joint in addition to clerking for her family's law firm in Amarillo, Texas and a boutique criminal defense and appellate law firm in Lubbock, Texas. She has practiced law in Texas for more than 30 years.

Carol works primarily in bankruptcy and bankruptcy litigation, as well as contested guardianship and probate litigation including fraud and breach of fiduciary duty cases. She is one of the Level 1 attorneys in Denton County, Texas who is appointed as an Attorney and/or Guardian ad Litem in high conflict or complex guardianship cases in Probate Court. She provides mediation services for private pay and court appointed cases, but also volunteers as a pro bono mediator for the Denton County Alternative Dispute Resolution Program (DCAP). She regularly is appointed as an Attorney ad Litem in mental health court in Denton County. She is no stranger to commercial and civil litigation. She also handles her own appellate work in all courts in which she practices.

Ms. Wolfram was graduated with honors from Texas Tech Law School in 1984. She has owned her own law practice for most of her career. Carol is the mother of four grown children and is now a proud grandmother. She feels blessed to be able to spend much of her weekly time that she has away from her law practice (and the majority of her vacation time) doing faith-based volunteer work both locally and internationally (including Mexico). She has been able to use her legal training and experience in various countries in Africa to help encourage, empower and equip African lawyers and judges to better advocate for the poor, as well as African women who are working to bring peace and economic stability to their families and communities. Ms. Wolfram is a published author including the development of a systematic approach to Bible interpretation for lay persons, and several self-published books of fictional short stories.

OH WHAT A RELIEF
CHAPTER 7 CAN BE
By Carol Lynn Wolfram

Who Do You Help?

I help single and married individuals in the North Texas area who for a variety of reasons cannot pay all of their debt and provide for themselves and their families at the same time, and who qualify to file for chapter 7 bankruptcy protection. Typical reasons that stop people from being able to pay to keep up with their debts can be the loss of a job, the death of a spousal wage earner, divorce, health problems within the family, loss of business, unforeseen catastrophes like fire, extended or multiple armed services deployment(s), and other reasons. If they cannot work through their financial problems outside of bankruptcy, I help them file for chapter 7 bankruptcy and work with them throughout the process until they have received the full extent of debt relief and protection against bill collectors that they can get (this debt relief is called a discharge).

Individuals can qualify to file for chapter 7 bankruptcy (and avoid the payment plans of 3 – 5 years in a chapter 13) based upon their average monthly income over the last 6 months before they file for bankruptcy. Your income generally must be less than the levels of income for the area of the country in which you live which are published by the federal government for the size of family that you have when you file. The level of income is higher if you are married or if you have dependents (and how many dependents you have). These amounts are adjusted by the government periodically, so it is important to know what the levels are before you file. Individuals also can qualify to file for chapter 7 if more than 50% of their debt is "non consumer debt" – that means that more than half of your debt was incurred because you were trying to make a profit (e.g., run a business). Sometimes if you have extraordinary expenses which usually are outside of your control, you can qualify for chapter 7 even though your household income is higher than the published levels for the size of your family.

Common Bankruptcy Protection Obstacles

Many of my clients try to do just about anything and everything they can to prevent having to file for bankruptcy. Often they use their retirement funds to pay bills, or take out an equity loan on their houses. Sometimes they borrow money from family members. They make these sacrifices with the best of intentions because they want to honor their commitments to pay their debts.

Sometimes my clients delay talking to a bankruptcy lawyer because they are continuing to borrow money to help one or more of their children or aging parents.

Another reason that many of my clients wait as long as possible to speak to a bankruptcy lawyer is because they feel ashamed of themselves or their circumstances.

Because of unfair pressures from society or sometimes their own families and friends, they feel that they must be morally terrible people if they file for bankruptcy.

Sadly, sometimes they delay talking to a bankruptcy lawyer because of unethical bill collectors who threaten them with jail, or going after their houses or even other family members if they don't pay their debts. In the last few years, I have had more and more clients tell me that different bill collectors have told them that they will be arrested and go to jail if they don't make their bill payments.

Overcoming Chapter 7 Obstacles

I admit to my clients that there is no such thing as worry free bankruptcy. All of my clients worry. Part of my job as their lawyer is to help them worry a lot less and help them through the process so that for most of them the worry disappears as the case goes along.

I keep a box of tissue on my conference room table because I always like to tell my clients that no matter what they have heard from their creditors, their friends or families, and sometimes even their spiritual leaders, filing for bankruptcy does not mean that they are terrible people. I tell them that bankruptcy is such an important right that it is a part of our US Constitution (Article I, Section 8).

At least two of the men (James Wilson and Robert Morris) who signed the Constitution spent time in debtors' prison, and many others who were influential in the early days of our country suffered greatly with debts that they couldn't pay (including Jefferson and Washington). Lots of good people and lots of famous people have needed debt relief.

I also like to tell my clients that the concept of debt forgiveness goes all the way back to the Old Testament in the Bible, where the Israelites were commanded to forgive debt between themselves every 7 years, and every 50 years all real property was to be returned to the family who had the original land grant, so forgiveness is part of the heart of God.

I give my clients permission to let their children grow up and take care of themselves. Taking care of adult children who need help should not always mean bailing them out financially.

I also tell my clients that if they come into money down the road, the Bankruptcy Code specifically allows for the voluntary repayment of discharged debts (11 USC 524(f)). If they feel a moral obligation or heartfelt desire to repay one or more of their debts, they have the freedom to repay none, some or all of their debts, but their creditors cannot ask them to do so.

Many of my clients cry with relief when I tell them these things, which is why I have the tissues out on my conference room table. Most of these folks eventually file for bankruptcy and are able to have a fresh start, most of them are able to save their houses if they have one, and their cars, household furnishings and retirement if they have any, their stress levels go way down, and they have a lot more peace in their lives.

Common Misconceptions Surrounding Chapter 7

The most common misconceptions that my clients have generally relate to what kinds of debts can be discharged and what kinds of property still have to be paid for even though they file for bankruptcy protection.

The most common types of debt that generally won't be discharged are student loans, taxes, domestic support obligations, and obligations to a spouse, former spouse or child arising from a divorce decree or court order. There are some exceptions to some of these categories, but they depend upon the specific facts of each case. Sometimes they require a lawsuit to be filed by the clients inside of their bankruptcy case which the clients must win in order to get those kinds of debts discharged.

It is also very important to know that debts that are not listed – either because someone didn't want to put that debt into the case or because it was forgotten or just unknown – do not get discharged. (You have to file your paperwork under penalty of perjury, so intentionally

www.ingramcontent.com/pod-product-compliance
Lightning Source LLC
Chambersburg PA
CBHW071528200326
41519CB00019B/6107

At least two of the men (James Wilson and Robert Morris) who signed the Constitution spent time in debtors' prison, and many others who were influential in the early days of our country suffered greatly with debts that they couldn't pay (including Jefferson and Washington). Lots of good people and lots of famous people have needed debt relief.

I also like to tell my clients that the concept of debt forgiveness goes all the way back to the Old Testament in the Bible, where the Israelites were commanded to forgive debt between themselves every 7 years, and every 50 years all real property was to be returned to the family who had the original land grant, so forgiveness is part of the heart of God.

I give my clients permission to let their children grow up and take care of themselves. Taking care of adult children who need help should not always mean bailing them out financially.

I also tell my clients that if they come into money down the road, the Bankruptcy Code specifically allows for the voluntary repayment of discharged debts (11 USC 524(f)). If they feel a moral obligation or heartfelt desire to repay one or more of their debts, they have the freedom to repay none, some or all of their debts, but their creditors cannot ask them to do so.

Many of my clients cry with relief when I tell them these things, which is why I have the tissues out on my conference room table. Most of these folks eventually file for bankruptcy and are able to have a fresh start, most of them are able to save their houses if they have one, and their cars, household furnishings and retirement if they have any, their stress levels go way down, and they have a lot more peace in their lives.

Common Misconceptions Surrounding Chapter 7

The most common misconceptions that my clients have generally relate to what kinds of debts can be discharged and what kinds of property still have to be paid for even though they file for bankruptcy protection.

The most common types of debt that generally won't be discharged are student loans, taxes, domestic support obligations, and obligations to a spouse, former spouse or child arising from a divorce decree or court order. There are some exceptions to some of these categories, but they depend upon the specific facts of each case. Sometimes they require a lawsuit to be filed by the clients inside of their bankruptcy case which the clients must win in order to get those kinds of debts discharged.

It is also very important to know that debts that are not listed – either because someone didn't want to put that debt into the case or because it was forgotten or just unknown – do not get discharged. (You have to file your paperwork under penalty of perjury, so intentionally leaving out debts or property is not an option. Being careless and not working to find out who all of your creditors are is not an option either.)

Less common debts for which a discharge can be denied are fraud, breach of fiduciary duty (such as misbehaving using a Power of Attorney or acting as a trustee of a trust), intentional injury to another person or another person's property, injury or death to a person caused while driving drunk or high, loans made against retirement funds, among others. Some of these kinds of debts are denied discharge pretty much automatically. Some of these kinds of debts require the creditors to file a lawsuit and object to the discharge of their debts.

When clients file for bankruptcy, they get to claim certain types of property as exempt, which means that the property cannot be taken from them and sold off to pay their creditors. The property has to be listed in their bankruptcy paperwork, and fair market values have to be given for all of that property. Then, depending upon where the individuals live and whether they are single or married, there are limits on what kinds of property can be claimed as exempt, and how much of that property can be exempt based on how much it is worth. For many of my clients, all of their property qualifies as exempt property because their property consists of their home, car, household furnishings, clothing and inexpensive jewelry, all of which fall under the dollar caps for those categories.

Generally speaking, if you are paying for exempt property in installment payments and the property has not been paid for completely when you file for bankruptcy, you have to keep making the payments or you can lose the property. In other words, you can't keep your house if you still owe money on it and stop making payments even if you file for bankruptcy. The same is true for your car, and sometimes for furniture, appliances, computers and other items. It is important for your lawyer to know all of your property for which you are still making payments so that you can decide if you want to keep that property, and if you can afford to keep that property.

Sometimes, you have to sign an agreement with a creditor after you file for bankruptcy that says you agree to keep paying for the property and if you don't the bankruptcy doesn't count for that creditor. Those kinds of agreements are called reaffirmation agreements, and are common agreements for cars, furniture and appliances. Reaffirmation agreements are serious contracts. If you stop paying after the agreement becomes final and the creditor repossesses and sells the property, but it is not enough to pay what you owe, the creditor can still collect the difference from you. However, if you don't agree to sign a reaffirmation agreement, you very well may lose your car or your furniture.

Avoiding Chapter 7 Pitfalls and Mistakes

The most important pitfall to avoid is failing to tell your lawyer everything about your debts and your property. I can't help clients work through secret problems. In a worst case scenario, keeping secrets can cause the clients to lose their discharge, which is the goal of everyone who files for bankruptcy.

For individuals, I would tell you not to empty out your retirement funds or take out home equity loans to pay creditors, hoping to stay out of bankruptcy – those are exempt assets that the law says are for your fresh start and that you are entitled to shield from most creditors.

It is important to remember that you have to pay your bills going forward after you file for bankruptcy. In a chapter 7, whatever debts you make after the date and time that you file your case do not receive a discharge. You cannot file for bankruptcy again for at least 8 years unless you qualify for an exception. Two of the schedules that you have to complete with your bankruptcy paperwork are income and expense schedules. You need to look at those schedules very carefully. If you cannot pay your monthly bills going forward, then you either have to increase your income or reduce your expenses. If you don't, you can lose your car, cell phone, or end up homeless even though you received a discharge in bankruptcy.

Common Fears About Filing for Chapter 7 Bankruptcy

Some of my clients have judgments or lawsuits against them when they file for bankruptcy, and they worry that those won't go away. Most of the time they do go away. If a judgment has been filed in real property records, it generally can be avoided or set aside. Lawsuits that haven't gone to judgment yet have to stop when the bankruptcy is filed and can't move forward again unless that creditor goes to the bankruptcy court and gets permission. Most of the time, that permission is not granted.

One of the most frequent fears that I hear from my clients is the fear that they will never be able to rebuild their credit. After all, bankruptcy stays on your credit report for ten years. However, for most of my clients, it is not that hard to rebuild credit. In fact, many of them start getting "pre-approved" credit card offers in the mail starting shortly after they receive their discharge. There are companies who specialize in car loans to people who have filed for bankruptcy. The interest rates may be higher, but not always. You can qualify for apartment or house leases, or even buy a house after bankruptcy. Not always right away, but you need to get to a place where you can safely make those payments anyway before you jump into that scenario again.

One fear that I do want my clients to have is a fear of easy, post bankruptcy credit. That can get them into trouble quickly, and you can stay in trouble for a long time because of it. I generally tell my clients to throw those pre-approved credit card offers in the recycle bin without even opening them. One of the best things you can do after bankruptcy for yourself and your family is to live within your means.

Why File for Chapter 7?

The goal for every person who can and does file for chapter 7 protection is to receive the court order that grants that person a discharge of all of the debts that can be discharged.

A discharge is available to honest debtors for them to be able to make what the courts call a "fresh start." That means that they can move forward to work and protect their families without the burden of debt that they cannot pay, and without the fear that creditors can freeze or empty their bank accounts, file lawsuits against them, or hassle them at work or at home with collection calls and letters.

The vast majority of my clients experience a great sense of relief twice while their case is active. The first feeling of relief happens when the case and all the paperwork required to go with it are filed, and they know that their creditors are under a court order to stop collection actions without bankruptcy court permission (which won't be granted without good cause). The second feeling of relief is when they receive the court order of discharge. Their peace of mind returns. They stop being afraid to answer the telephone when it rings. They don't feel they have to cash their paychecks and stay away from bank accounts because their creditors are looking to get access to their money. Their paychecks actually go to pay monthly bills instead of high interest rates on credit cards that are maxed out.

What Led You to The Field of Bankruptcy Law?

The answer to that question is a funny story.

When I was in law school, I was certain that I wanted to practice primarily in the areas of consumer law and maybe personal injury. I was sure that I would just hate bankruptcy law. My first job as a lawyer was in 1984. I was hired originally to do consumer law. Then, on my first day of work as a "real lawyer," one of my bosses came in and said that the firm had just been hired to represent several debtor companies in an oil and gas reorganization case, and they were going to have me be one of the primary lawyers on those cases. I was shocked! However, I quickly came to love the field of bankruptcy law, and I have been working in that area ever since.

Final Thoughts and Next Steps

Get legal advice from a bankruptcy lawyer sooner – don't make getting legal advice about bankruptcy as the last thing on your list to help you with your debt problems; you might find that you have other alternatives, or you might find that if you need to file, you can do so more successfully than you imagine.

If someone needs help with chapter 7 individual bankruptcy case, what's the best way for them to connect with you?

If you feel that you need help with chapter 7, then before I can talk with you or meet with you, I need to have the complete list of your creditors. Reason being, I am required to check and see if I have any conflicts of interest. It's not usually the case, however, I am required to check every time.

Once we've cleared that formality, then, I will ask you some preliminary questions to see if it looks like you qualify for chapter 7. If it appears that you do qualify, then we can schedule a free consultation at my office. If you live in the North Texas area, you can contact me in any of the following ways:

Email me at clwolframlegal@gmail.com or carol@clwolframlegal.com. Call me at (940) 321-0019. Visit my website at www.clwolframlegal.com and email me from there. Visit my Avvo profile at https://www.avvo.com and email me from there.

CHRISTOPHER J. KANE

Attorney, Christopher J. Kane, PC
Portland, Oregon

Email: chris@ckanelaw.com

Website: https://ckanelaw.com

LinkedIn: Christopher J. Kane, P.C

Avvo Attorney Profile: Christopher J Kane

Facebook: @ckanelaw

Call: (503) 380-7822

Christopher J. Kane grew up in Oregon and earned his bachelor's degree in Economics from Portland State University in 1991. After earning his Juris Doctor degree from Northwestern School of Law at Lewis & Clark College in 1994, Kane became a member of the Oregon State Bar in 1995.

From 2001 to 2005 he worked as an associate attorney with Snyder & Associates, a prominent firm that focused solely on consumer bankruptcy and progressed to open his own practice in Northeast Portland, in 2005. His primary focus has been on helping consumers and small business tackle their debts and get a fresh start in their financial lives.

Kane has always focused on helping "the little guy." Helping them is where he gets his professional satisfaction. He has represented thousands of individuals and small businesses in both state and federal courts, and in many areas of the law. These include Social Security disability law, landlord/tenant relations, employment law, consumer protection law, estate planning, business entity formation and consulting, and bankruptcy.

Kane's primary focus since 2001 has been on bankruptcy law, specifically in helping find debt relief solutions for individuals and small businesses, and also works with clients in the areas of business law, estate planning, and real estate investment transactions.

CHAPTER 7 vs CHAPTER 13 BANKRUPTCY
By Christopher J. Kane

Who Do You Help?

I represent people all over the state of Oregon, most of my clients are from the Portland Metro area but I do have clients all over the state and I can help anybody in the state of Oregon. My clients comprise every walk of life you could possibly imagine, but the one theme they all have in common is they're buried in debt, overwhelmed, not sure what they can do about it.

Sometimes they're facing a foreclosure on their home, their wages are being garnished, they've just been served a lawsuit, their car just got repossessed, and have those creditors calling all day long begging them for money. Often times as a result of reduction in their income, they've lost their job, just got through a divorce and find themselves deep in debt.

Medical problems are still a big huge issue even with the current Affordable Care Act, there are millions of people out there without any health insurance. You can go from zero debt to half a million dollars in debt in just a couple of days if you have a very serious medical condition.

Often times that debt can stick with them for a long time, so they come to me, we sit down, talk about their situation, and more often than not I can find a solution for them to move forward.

Chapter 7 vs Chapter 13 - Myths and Misconceptions

There are a ton of myths and misconceptions that people have around bankruptcy but as far as Chapter 7 versus Chapter 13 bankruptcy goes, the most common misconception I see, is a lot of people having the understanding that if they go through a Chapter 13 bankruptcy they're going to end up having to pay off 100% of their debt over a three to five year payment plan.

The most basic difference between a Chapter 7 and a Chapter 13 bankruptcy, is Chapter 7 takes about 90 days to complete where Chapter 13 takes a minimum of three years to a maximum of five years. Chapter 13 is more of a debt restructuring program where you're making payments to a bankruptcy trustee every month for a three to five year period of time. Those payments are then distributed amongst the creditors depending on the plan that gets confirmed by the court.

A lot of people think, "Oh no. I'm $50,000 in credit card debt. How can I pay that off in five years? I'm only making a couple grand a month and can barely put food on the table." But, the reality is the vast majority of people who do end up filing Chapter 13 bankruptcy do not end up paying even up to maybe 25% of their debt.

It depends on why they're going to Chapter 13 in the first place, what kinds of debts they have, what kinds of property are they trying to hold on to, whether it be a home, continue to pay the mortgage, continue to pay the car loan, keep the car. Whatever it is, there may be different reasons people can file Chapter 13 and choose to file Chapter 13 over a Chapter 7. Often times Chapter 13 can be a much better solution for people in the long run.

I'll give you an example of a client who was extremely overwhelmed and had a lot of misinformation about Chapter 13. They had about $50,000 of credit card debt but the main reason they came to see me is they lost their driver's license because they had about $7,000 of traffic tickets they hadn't paid. Here in the state of Oregon and in many states, if you don't pay your traffic tickets they'll eventually yank your license. This person needed to drive for work. They actually lost their job because of that. They were able to get re-employed somewhere else but they're main line of work was driving.

It turns out when you file a Chapter 13 bankruptcy you can actually discharge those traffic tickets, where in a Chapter 7 case you cannot, so in Chapter 13, you get your license back and can get rid of traffic tickets.

I got him into a monthly plan to pay the trustee $100 for 36 months for a total of $3,600. He was able to get rid of $57,000 worth of debt, get his driver's license back, get back to work in his chosen industry, get a fresh start and move forward… without costing a ton of money.

Unknown Pitfalls & Common Mistakes

Often times when people find themselves in debt one of the first things they try to do is to sell the assets they have, or try to hide them so that their creditors cannot come after those assets or find them. I would strongly suggest that if such thoughts are crossing your mind, go talk to a competent bankruptcy attorney before you do anything like that because chances are hiding assets prior to filing bankruptcy can end up being a bad deal for you.

It can end up causing you a lot of problems if you eventually do have to file bankruptcy and especially if you're not selling property for the full market value. If you're giving someone a deal or just giving your brother the car, transferring a title or anything else under somebody else's name, that can really backfire on you. I would say if you're finding yourself deep in debt and you're looking to do something like that, go talk to a professional first who can make sure you're not doing something that's going to bite you later on. That's a very common thing that I see.

Consequences of Non-Full Disclosure

The first thing people need to be reminded of is if they do not tell their lawyer everything, if you don't give your lawyer full disclosure, your lawyer can't effectively help you 100%. When you go to speak to an attorney, there's the attorney-client privilege and everything you tell your attorney is fully confidential. You decide who you're going to and what you're going to disclose. When you file a bankruptcy case and sign those documents before they get filed with the court, you're signing under penalty of perjury under federal law. If for some reason the bankruptcy trustee and/or the bankruptcy court finds out that you're lying about anything, you can go to jail. It can cost you a lot of money as well. You lose your discharge and there could potentially be an order that prevents you from ever filing bankruptcy again. I've seen those things happen before and it's not pretty.

The reason the why disclosure of assets is so important is when you file a bankruptcy, the bankruptcy trustee assigned to you in a Chapter 7 case, their main job is to see if you have any assets they can sell to get money for your creditors before you can start the process. We have exemptions that the state and federal law give you to protect each kind of asset up to a certain dollar value and protects the equity on those assets up to a certain level. So, if you have equity above and beyond the exemption amount then sometimes, Chapter 13's a way to hold on to those assets, or in Chapter 7, sometimes there are things we can do to help you hold on to those assets.

If you get rid of an asset, or you transfer an asset before you file bankruptcy, the trustee can go back as far as four years. If you transfer anything within four years prior to filing bankruptcy, in some circumstances they could reverse that transaction, get the property back from whoever you gave it to, sell the property, give money to creditors and the person you gave that property to or sold the property to, would lose that asset as well. As you can imagine, that alone can really cause you a lot of problems. So disclosure is extremely important for a number of different reasons; both to protect yourself, save yourself headaches as well as preventing yourself from getting into big trouble and obviously making your bankruptcy worthless if you lose your discharge.

I've seen some instances (none of my clients) where people have attempted to hide assets and not disclose everything with their lawyer in the hope of not being found out. Well, as bankruptcy trustees, you'd be surprised how many different ways they can find out what's going on. They can check all the public record. If you sold a house or sold a car and the title was effectively legally transferred, that is a matter of public record; anybody can find that out.

Also if there's anybody out there who knows about this situation, they know you filed bankruptcy, they could show up to the meeting and speak up saying, "Hey Mr. Trustee. I know this person just gave their car to their brother last week. It's worth about $10,000. You might want to go get that." I've seen that happen before. Again, not with any of my clients, but I've been sat there waiting for my turn and seen other people get busted right there in front of everybody in the room. It happens, and like I said, if that's found out, you could be subjected to some pretty severe penalties as well.

People think they can shield themselves from those things happening, but the trustees, they have their ways of finding out and sometimes people in your life who want to see you go down can find ways to help that happen.

Helping Clients to Achieve Their Goals

It gives me extreme personal and professional satisfaction to be a part of the transformation which takes place from when people come in to see me, at their wits end, overwhelmed and not knowing what to do, to being in a place where they have come out on top, feeling like they have a bright future ahead of them, putting the past behind them and moving forward.

I disclose to all my clients that I too filed a Chapter 7 bankruptcy back in 1998 when I was having a tough time. It was the first time I tried to be self-employed and didn't know what I was doing. I was able to file a Chapter 7 and get rid of some debt and move forward, and it was one of the best things I've ever done for myself. My clients really appreciate me telling them that because they understand that I've been there too.

I call myself the "Save the Little Guy" Lawyer. Everything that I've ever done in my legal career, has always been centered around helping working people. I grew up in a working class family, my parents didn't make a ton of money and we didn't live on a lot. I've been working, myself, since I was about 14 years old... It's not getting any easier here in this country for those of us who don't have millions of disposable dollars. A lot of people need a second chance and I'm glad that I can be a part of that.

There's no shame in being in the position of facing bankruptcy. Millions of people in this country have had to file bankruptcy in the last 10, 20 years. Some of the most successful entrepreneurs, quite a few of them have been through the process of filing bankruptcy. In fact, I would say probably nearly half of those people are going through bankruptcy. Sometimes you need to hit the bottom before you can get back to the top. Also you have to take chances in entrepreneurship and sometimes they don't work out the way you thought they were going to, however, you always have another chance to try it again.

The Winding Path

I'm often asked, "What led you to where you are today, were you destined to become Bankruptcy Attorney?" Well, I went to Portland State University here in Portland for my undergraduate degree. I actually went to college thinking I was going to pursue a career in electrical engineering because in high school I was always really into math and science and electronics and things like that. But I got into college, and once I got into calculus courses I realized I don't get this and I don't enjoy trying to get this.

I found myself taking a lot of sociology, economics, and social science classes and really enjoying them a lot. And it was a particular sociology professor of mine in college who took me aside one day, we were talking about a paper that I wrote that he gave me an A on, and he asked me, "Hey Chris, what are you going to do when you get out of school?"

"Well, I was going into engineering school and now I've decided not to go that direction, I really don't know where I'm headed right now."

He said," I think you should be a lawyer and I want to help you however I can to get into law school because you write like an attorney. You're obviously very concerned about socio-economic issues and about the plight of the common person."

He was the one who really inspired me to look into law school and I got accepted here at Lewis & Clark Law School here in Portland. I went there in '92, graduated in '94, passed the Bar exam in '95. When I came out of law school, the American Bar Association was telling us new lawyers, "This is the toughest job market we've seen in many, many, many years. Good luck out there."

I was out there doing a lot of volunteer work for attorneys and kind of learning the ropes and doing some contract work on this and that. I eventually opened up my own office downtown specializing in social security disability law when I first got started, which is a real tough way to go because you need a lot of cases in the pipeline to be able to pay the bills. I found myself digging into debt and 1998, I filed my own bankruptcy because I decided I needed a second chance.

I got myself a job at a bankruptcy law firm where we practiced exclusively in bankruptcy. That's all I did there for about four and a half years, and I left in 2005. Built my own office here in Northeast Portland, and I've been here ever since, practicing almost exclusively in bankruptcy. There are a few other things that I do as well but it's the majority of what I've been doing for a long, long time now.

Like I said, I grew up in a working class family. We never had a lot of money, so I knew what it was like to struggle and had to do what you had to do to make it by. So, I've been through some pitfalls in my own life, as we all have, so I really like to spend a lot of time with my clients building personal relationships to understand what they've been going through. It's really what sets me apart from a lot of people who do what I do. I'm willing to sit here and hear your story. I want to know you before I can really help you decide what's in your best interest.

Final Thoughts for the Little Guy

I always tell my clients and potential clients when they come into see me, if you leave my office feeling better about your situation and with a smile on your face, then we've been successful and I believe the vast majority of the time, people I meet with do leave my office with a smile on their face. There is always something we can do. There's always an option. There is a way out.

If you go to see a professional like myself early on in the case, before you really hit panic mode, that's definitely the best time. You can have a clear, open minded and discreet discussion about your situation before you do anything that's going to cause you problems like transferring an asset or anything else.

If you're thinking about doing something that just doesn't feel right, come and see me first. See a professional first to make sure you're not doing something that's going to cause you problems in the future. With proper planning, if you see a professional early on enough in your situation, then doing some proper planning before you file bankruptcy can save you a lot of money and a lot of headache. So the message is, the earlier you feel yourself heading into a spiraling hole of debt, go see an attorney and talk to a professional like myself who understands what you're going through, and remember, there is a way out. Don't wait until the final hour when you're in full panic mode.

Next Steps

If at this stage you feel you want to know more about the differences between Chapter 7 and Chapter 13 bankruptcies and how you get help for your own specific situation, the best thing to do first is you go to look at my website at https://ckanelaw.com. I have a lot of information on there about different types of bankruptcy, what I do and how I can help.

You can send me a message directly through the website asking me to give you a call and set a consultation. If you call my office, more often than not, I'm the one who's going to answer the phone, I'll set the appointment right there and see as soon as you want to. The office number is, (503)380-7822. I'm very easy to get a hold of and if I can't help you with what you need help with, I can always find somebody who can. Bankruptcy is not always the best option, sometimes people need some other advice and I can always send you to an appropriate professional who has the right advice for you.

DEEPALIE MILIE JOSHI, ESQ

Founder & Managing Attorney
Joshi Law Group, San Diego, CA

Email: milie@joshilawgroup.com

Website: https://www.joshilawgroup.com

LinkedIn: https://linkedin.com/in/joshilawgroup

Avvo Attorney Profile: Deepalie Milie Joshi

Facebook: @JoshiLawGroup

Twitter: @JoshiLawGroup

Call: (619) 822-7566

Ms. Joshi is the founder and managing attorney at Joshi Law Group. Ms. Joshi personally works on each and every case to ensure that a client's needs are being met to the fullest extent. Ms. Joshi learned very early in her legal career that an attorney's integrity is just as important as an attorney's competence, reputation, and breadth of knowledge. Ms. Joshi founded Joshi Law Group on these principles.

Ms. Joshi's passion for the law and her desire to help people are what drive her towards excellence. Ms. Joshi made the decision to become an attorney at a very young age and worked diligently to become an attorney licensed in two states by the age of 25. After growing up in a small town in Tennessee, Ms. Joshi graduated from Vanderbilt University with a Bachelor of Arts in 2006.

She then went on to earn her law degree from Thomas Jefferson School of Law. Ms. Joshi is licensed to practice law in the State of Tennessee, the State of California, the U.S. District Courts of the Southern District of California, the Central District of California, and the Northern District of California. She is also a member of number of local and statewide attorney groups for litigation and bankruptcy.

Outside of the law, Ms. Joshi enjoys spending time with her husband and family, yoga, swimming, following the NBA, and reading about history.

COMMON MISTAKES WHEN BANKRUPTCY IS UNAVOIDABLE
By Deepalie Milie Joshi

What Kinds of People Do You Work With?

This is a trick question, because I think there's an assumption that there is a certain or specific type of person or kind of person that usually ends up in a bankruptcy attorney's office. Usually, my clients are all types of people, all types of professions, everyday people, blue-collar workers, white-collar workers, just sometimes life happens. For those who are not financially prepared or have depleted their financial resources after being financially prepared, sometimes bankruptcy ends up being the only option.

One of the first things that we deal with is this preconceived shame. Folks who come in to talk to me are often in a place where they're feeling shameful, feeling that they've somehow failed, and that this is their only saving grace. In reality, bankruptcy may be on the horizon a lot sooner than those feelings emerge.

Common Misconceptions

One of the common misconceptions is that you have to deplete all of your resources before considering bankruptcy as an option. For example, a lot of people use up their retirement funds. Tap out their IRA or their 401K, and those are completely protectable funds when you go through a Chapter 7 or Chapter 13 Bankruptcy.

In my experience, this misconception often comes from this American value of self-reliance. Where you don't really talk to people about being in debt, because there's some sort of shame around it.

Most people don't tell their friends and family if they have more money going out every month than they have coming in. If they do it's in a joking and lighthearted way. Typically, not in a serious fashion where, "Hey, I'm in trouble. My credit card debt is out of control." Or, "Hey, I'm in trouble. I don't know how I'm going to make rent next month."

People usually don't talk about those serious problems. When those problems start to accumulate over time, then they start taking desperate actions like cashing out the 401K they've been building for 20 years, or borrowing money from family members that they don't know how they're going to be able to pay back.

Getting Finances in Order

I once had a family come to me to talk about bankruptcy. They were your stereotypical American family in that they had their own home, 2.4 kids, a couple of dogs, a couple of kids, wife worked part-time, husband worked full-time. The economy had been tough, and the husband had been getting fewer hours at work.

While in the heyday of the economic boom, he was making lots of money with overtime and there was more work that could be done. Over the past 10 years, the availability for work had depleted. There were times where he was laid off for a few months at a time, or where he was only partially employed.

Basically, with the home, the car, the kids, the dogs, there's a set number of expenses that have to go out every month. When the income is not coming in, eventually, that negative net accrued. After a couple of years, they had no idea how they were going to catch up. Behind on a couple of mortgage payments, behind on a car payment, only making minimum payments on credit cards, and as a last ditch effort, depleted a $30,000 401K account, which incurred tax debt, so then tax debt was piled on top of that.

When they came to see me, the one thing that I really had wished was that they had come to see me six months earlier. If they had come in sooner, I would have been able to advise them on what bills to actually not pay. It's one thing to not be able to pay your bills at all, and another thing to be hanging on by the minimum payment.

If that minimum payment is causing you to fall behind on substantial debts, like your mortgage or your car, then I think you're in a position where you need to talk to a bankruptcy attorney to prioritize which debts need to be paid first and which ones need to be dealt with by some sort of larger authority, such as the bankruptcy court. Eventually, we were able to help them get their finances in order, but the process was a lot more complicated than it would have been had they come to see me six months earlier.

Common Pitfalls and Mistakes

Depending on your state's exemption laws and whether or not they follow their state laws or the federal exemption laws, the property that you have is usually safe. One of the biggest mistakes or pitfalls is assuming that if you file for bankruptcy someone's going to come and take all of your stuff. That's not true. There are lots of legal protections in place to protect, basically, your core needs, so that you have something to start over with when your debts are wiped clean.

Throughout my career as a Bankruptcy Attorney, I'm often asked, "What's the most important to you about being able to help your clients to avoid common pitfalls and or mistakes which prevent them from achieving their goals?" To which my answer is always the same, "Being able to give them a fresh start is most important to me because truly, that's what bankruptcy is."

Being able to take a person, a family, a couple, or a business even, who see no way forward with all the problems around them, and being able to guide them through that process and allowing them to come up for a fresh breath of air, and see the future, hope for the future, and plan for the future again, that fresh start is satisfying for me every single time. It makes me feel like I've kept my soul a little bit longer being an attorney. It's a profession that can very easily lead you to have a bit of darkness grow within your soul. In that sense it makes me feel like I'm actually helping people and doing some good in the world. It's my own personal way of fighting against institutions that I think are not always fair to the average person. Fighting against them is important to me.

For example, credit card companies, they tend to target young students, college freshmen. They have booths set up all over college freshmen orientation areas. They're soliciting these 18-year-olds, who are essentially kids, who don't know anything about finances, because they don't teach it in high school. They're soliciting these kids to sign up for credit cards with 20 to 30% interest rates on them. They're often successful which just starts this cycle of credit and debt that is very difficult to overcome, unless you have a substantial form of income, or a family member who's able to bail you out of that situation.

My Journey to Becoming a Bankruptcy Attorney

I knew I wanted to be an attorney when I was very young. I got bit by the bug in, and it burrowed in and made me follow the legal path every step of the way. I did my undergraduate studies at Vanderbilt University and then went to law school in San Diego immediately thereafter. I earned my J.D. in two and a half years, and then went on to get licensed in the state of California and also the state of Tennessee, which is where I'm from.

I started practicing as a bankruptcy attorney right away, as soon as I was licensed. Primarily in California, because at the time California was especially experiencing a rather high percentage of bankruptcy filings with the concurrent housing crisis that had happened a couple of years earlier and was continuing to unfold.

At the time I started practicing, there were a lot of bankruptcy laws that were being tested by the current economic situation. The law was rapidly evolving and changing, and there were new tools that were developing to be able to help people in debt, and new laws that were unfolding that actually hurt people in debt, if they didn't go about bankruptcy the right way.

As soon as I started practicing, bankruptcy, the law piqued my interest, and it continues to. I just find the law, endlessly fascinating, and its ability to help people is the icing on the cake. I worked for a bankruptcy firm where I handled hundreds of cases. After a year, I decided to be brave enough to hang my own shingle and start Joshi Law Group.

Final Thoughts

Two things I tell every single client that has ever come into my office, the first is whatever you think is going on, I've seen worse. That is almost always true. There's the one that's always the worst, but 99 out of 100 times, when someone is sitting in front of me, and they're telling me how bad things have gotten, I'm there to tell you, "Look, I've seen worse and I've fixed worse."

People often think their situation is unique which goes along with that feeling of shame, holding it inside of yourself for so long, and the consequent problems as a result of not being able to deal with them. You build this protective shell around yourself where everything outside of that shell is bad and terrible, and you don't know how to deal with it. Coming out and actually talking to somebody about it is usually a very cathartic step.

The second point is there's no judgment. Seriously, if you come and talk to me about what's going on, I have no judgments. You're in a bad situation, and I'm here to help you. Don't think that I'm going to be judging you while you're sharing your current situation with me. The concept of being judged plays havoc with may people, which is understandable and all more reason to ensure you're talking to an attorney you feel comfortable with.

Bankruptcy can give you a fresh start, but also it balances the rights of debtors, those seeking a fresh start, and creditors. As many people as there are that really did just fall on bad times and need help in starting over, there are also folks that abuse the system, commit fraud, and then seek protection from the bankruptcy court. For those reasons, the bankruptcy court does balance the rights of debtors and creditors.

If you feel you'd like to know more about avoiding common mistakes when bankruptcy is unavoidable, you can find me at https://www.joshilawgroup.com on Facebook, Twitter, and LinkedIn.

JYOTHI PALLAPOTHU

Bankruptcy Attorney
Law Office of Jyothi Pallapothu

Email: jyothi@jplegalillinois.com

Website: http://jplegalillinois.com

LinkedIn: https://linkedin.com/in/jyothipallapothu

Facebook: https://www.facebook.com/jplegalillinois

Call: (312) 496-3326 | **Fax:** (312) 496-3326

Jyothi Pallapothu has extensive experience in foreclosure law and related real estate issues. During law school, Jyothi served as a law clerk to a prominent local attorney where she cultivated her passion for helping individuals.

After law school, she served as a judicial clerk to the Hon. Gale B. Robinson in the General Sessions Court of Metro-Davidson County in Nashville, TN and volunteered at the ACLU of Nashville, TN.

Jyothi found her way to Chicago after passing the Illinois bar where she began her career working in various consumer rights firms. As a passionate advocate for the individual, she works hard to make sure her clients are well represented in court.

BANKRUPTCY AND THE FORECLOSURE PROCESS
By Jyothi Pallapothu

Who Do You Help?

With my background and the type of law that I do, I mainly represent the individual. I do foreclosure defense. It's primarily homeowners who are facing the loss of their home and I defend them and we work on different ways where we can try to save their home and one of the options is usually bankruptcy.

When it comes to the foreclosure process and bankruptcy, I the common misconception I see on a regular basis is that homeowners think that if they file bankruptcy that everything's wiped out, the debt is wiped out and that they can keep the home for free. That's the biggest obstacle when helping the people I work with. I have to spend time explaining that just because you file bankruptcy does not mean you get a free home.

When people are faced with the loss of their home, when they miss a few payments on their mortgage, they start getting all the documents, the letters, maybe some court documents. Illinois is considered a judicial foreclosure state, meaning that before a bank can foreclose on a property they have to go to the court process. That can take some time. I have, the homeowners that come to me and depending on what their goal is, whether they want to keep the property or not, we have different strategies.

Worry-Free Bankruptcy | 83

Getting Results

When homeowners want to keep their property, one of the things I can do is discuss bankruptcy. One of the biggest hurdles and the most common that I see is that they are thinking, okay I filed Chapter 7, now all my debts are wiped out. In cases like that, I have to tell them that, when you sign a mortgage and when you take money out and sign a note, there are two different aspects of it. When you're buying a home, yes you sign a note. That attaches to the money the bank gives you to buy the home, but then the home is used as collateral that the bank holds onto until you pay back that loan.

What a bankruptcy does in Chapter 7 is to wipe out the money aspect of it so you don't owe the bank anything but then that house is still there. What do we do with that house? The bank can still foreclose on the house, it's just that you won't owe any money on the house once the foreclosure is done. There's a possibility you don't owe any money but you can still lose your home.

What bankruptcy does and what I have to explain to my clients is that, yes you filed bankruptcy, but you still have to do what's called a loan modification because let's face it there's no such thing as a free house. A loan modification is working with the bank to restructure the loan where you had the money you took out and that way you can work on getting into a new agreement with the bank, the foreclosure process goes away and you continue making your payments. So what a foreclosure does is that it's forcing the banks hand to restructure that loan that you have, that way they can't take the house away from you and you still continue to pay.

Also, one of my other concerns about clients and this is once again a very common thing where they couldn't afford the loan in the first place, have missed a couple years of payments are in foreclosure, have interest fees and late payment fees added on and are in a position where their debts are even more. But because of the way the bank restructures it and the fact that going with their Chapter 7 example, all the other debts are wiped out, that frees up some money where the bank can say, "Hey okay, your credit card debt was wiped out, your medical bills were wiped out. You have more money that you can put towards the mortgage and so you have an income that you can afford." That is probably the best example of how bankruptcy can affect a foreclosure.

Why Full Disclosure is Important

Let's image for a moment that you're a homeowner looking at the prospects of losing your home and wanting to take on the services of a bankruptcy lawyer to represent your case, however, and I've seen this before, you're a very private person who thinks, "I'm paying this attorney some good money, why should I tell her everything? Why should I give her full disclosure? Do I really need to tell her every single detail?" Well, if that sounds remotely like you, then allow me to share what could be the repercussions of withholding information.

Firstly, it's important for you to know that the lawyer-client relationship is based on confidentiality. One of the main things I tell my clients is, "I do not talk about your case, I don't release any information. The way I can represent my clients effectively is if they tell me everything. There's nothing to be embarrassed about." I say that to my clients a lot of times because when they come in, they're ashamed that they've reached a point in their lives where they can't pay their bills.

I tell them, "It's not shameful. The United States Federal Courts call the bankruptcy process, 'A fresh start.' I tell them, "It's a positive way of thinking. There was a recession where a lot of people were affected and the repercussions are still continuing from that recession." Simply put, "If the courts call it, 'A fresh start.' then you can look at it that way as well. Nobody's judging you, there's nothing to be ashamed about, embarrassed about and combined with the fact that there's confidentiality, I have to have all the information."

Now on the other hand, if I don't have all the information that I request, I can't effectively represent them because there may be some things in the bankruptcy process that I need to know and if they feel like they can't tell

Unknown Foreclosure Pitfalls

One unknown pitfall is it's not always a guarantee. A lot of times bankruptcy can help, but sometimes you just don't have enough money to get a loan modification even with all your debts wiped out, or maybe you're not making enough income. Whatever the case, bankruptcy is always the last choice to wipe away everything. There's always a few subset of individuals that just don't fall under the qualifications for Chapter 7 or Chapter 13 and they may have to lose their house.

I sometimes I have to tell them, "Look, there's something else that can be done." I try to be honest and make my clients aware that there's no guarantee that filing bankruptcy will save their home. That's the biggest pitfall that you have to understand. Filing bankruptcy does not cure all your woes. There's always that possibility that it won't really help you.

Why I'm a Bankruptcy Attorney

I've been practicing as a bankruptcy attorney since 2009. Illinois was one of the hardest hit as far as foreclosures. After eight, nine years practicing bankruptcy I look at every day as a new day where I'm helping, educating and putting people's fears at ease. It makes the day go by easier knowing that I'm helping people to not be afraid of what to expect, and that I can actually help them save their home and make them happy.

If anyone was to ask if helping people to face their fears of losing their homes is important to me, my answer would be , Yes, of course!" I guess I'm very pragmatic in the sense that I feel they should not put their head in the sand. People get bills, they don't want to open them. It is traumatizing and scary but I'm here to walk them through the process because I don't want them to lose their home. So many people have lost homes because they were uneducated or afraid and I'm here to hold their hands and make them understand what they can do. And if there's no option left and they have to lose their home, I'm here to tell them that too, but at the end of the day, I guide them and let them know how much time they have, and what else they can do. They always have an option, so they're never going in blindly with me.

How I Became a Bankruptcy Attorney

I went to law school at Thomas Cooley Law School in Michigan and ended up taking and passing the bar exam in Illinois. When I passed the bar it was November 2009, the recession had started and within two weeks of my first job I was given a caseload of foreclosures. I was just thrown in and so had to figure it out and it was mostly self-taught and when you learn yourself you retain that information more. That's how I started and that's how

I've stayed in the area. I haven't really branched out into any other areas, so I've become very familiar with how the laws have changed, how judges view different cases and I feel like I've been so steady in just one area, that I've become pretty proficient in assisting homeowners.

Final Thoughts

The best piece of information I can share is the minute you feel like you're going to fall behind on a payment, or the minute you feel that your bills are overwhelming you and you can't make those payments anymore, contact an attorney. There are plenty of attorneys out there that will sit down with and provide a quick overview without charging, thereby helping you to make decisions on how to proceed. That way, whether you want to file bankruptcy, go through the court process or work with the bank, you're not wasting too much time and falling further behind in debt.

Having said that, if you a homeowner wanting to know more about how bankruptcy can affect and impact the foreclosure process in Illinois, then you can definitely connect with me through my website, http://.JPLegalIllinois.com where you can use the online form to submit any questions, or call us on (312) 496-3326

ABOUT THE AUTHOR

Mark Imperial is a Best Selling Author, Syndicated Business Columnist, Syndicated Radio Host, and internationally recognized Stage, Screen, and Radio Host of numerous business shows spotlighting leading experts, entrepreneurs, and business celebrities.

His passion is discovering noteworthy business owners, professionals, experts and leaders who do great work, and sharing their stories and secrets to their success with the world on his syndicated radio program titled, "Remarkable Radio".

Mark is also the media marketing strategist and voice for some of the world's most famous brands. You can hear his voice over the airwaves weekly on Chicago radio and worldwide on iHeart Radio.

Mark is a Karate black belt, teaches kickboxing, loves Thai food, House Music, and his favorite TV show is infomercials.

Learn more:

www.MarkImperial.com
www.ImperialAction.com
www.RemarkableRadioShow.com